Partner, Orchard, Day Moon

Michael Todd Steffen

Červená Barva Press
Somerville, Massachusetts

Červená Barva Press
P.O. Box 440357
W. Somerville, MA 02144-3222

www.cervenabarvapress.com

Bookstore: www.thelostbookshelf.com

Cover Art: Irene Koronas

Cover Design: William J. Kelle

ISBN: 978-0-9883713-2-3

Library of Congress: 2013953562

In memory

Gary Mackin

1948 - 2012

TABLE OF CONTENTS

Partner, Orchard, Day Moon

Christmas in August

Wandering lost through the department stores
You catch a glimpse of yourself in an odd
Mirror gliding over the escalator's
Handrest—when the metal step slips forward
And you stumble, up walking around the mannequins
Clad for autumn in pullovers and cords.
Summer hasn't ended. As one begins
To fit a season, comfort stops to look
Ahead of what you're feeling. Just in jeans,
Tee-shirt and milemore loafers you are struck
Dumb by the bland forms' plush apparel, seeing
School buses, foliage turning mauve, a break
From the salad days. Small wonder marketing
Keeps shuffling our closets and our drawers
Outstripping the wind's transparent robe, still being
With the bag people, time on hand, indoors.

In Olinger, PA

The map I followed for my weekends there
Figured the hand shape of a maple leaf
With its New England autumn signature
Of woods and steeples, nineteenth century life

All knee deep, reading on to walk the town,
In Walgreens, parking lots, the politics
Of burning bras and music on the lawn,
Love of tennis and the open sacks

That Halloween to welcome porches brought.
To think I'd meet the more than meets the eye
Blinking through steam—the mayor clearing his throat
Beside me in the shower at the Y

Weirdly inviting me to the rehearsal
For a speech of his day's declaration
Declining still the upper for the middle
Neighborhoods where dog and rabbit run.

The Garden in the Ceiling

All you need are these suggestions
From an open window's box of upward blue,
The hung house plant climbing on its vine
Around the chain to the plaster on the ceiling
Trowel-swept in abstract arcs to lead the eye
To everything it has seen happen
Over again from the beginning—

A serpent coiling around a tree. Look up.
Painted among the angels in the garden
She has been teased out of him sunk
Still in the slumber of his dream of her
And the snake like a shadow clutches
To this tree's appeal to be harvested anyway

Then in shame they're fenced from paradise
And here's the shipbuilder in the flooded peaks
If you've found the beginning in
The middle of the ceiling just behind
The innocent creature holding out his finger
To the graven
Father in the cloud tuft (are they pointing
Authorship at each other?), close enough their energies
Merge like cloud and tree shadows...

Won't you come down?—

You shy to repeat to the suspended
Figures each with a promise hovering over you
In the ache of being here, still, just breathing.

Feathers

Feathers from my uncles' hunting blind
Were given to us kids for our straw hats.
You stuck the quill into the brim's cloth band.
Some called it *macaroni*. Others *belfry*.
The iridescence of the teal made me
Stare to blankness. It was like glass and wore
The appeal to land chance dice on. At the gunshots
I glanced up and the sky turned gray and sorry.

There was the time we came down to the stream
And found the wood duck snared in fishing nylon.
It took the bolt out of their careful aim
And walked down with a knife to cut the line
While our warm gung ho hounds circled and whined
Curious about this difference from the grounded.

Thanksgiving

One of my uncles shot the dinner goose
Out of the heavy sky of our providing.
Especially we bowed our heads for grace.
The drop accused him from the blinded sighting
Between the wince of killing and an old need.
With hands like walnut he was sensitive.
He tasted the salt of pain in gratitude.
One creature went silent. He went on to live
And join the toast at the table with its ornaments
For the holiday, the straw weft cornucopia
Basket with squash and gourds and native corn,
Auburn of oat sheaf in the candle's aura
Hushed for the dishes my aunt told us to pass
With sneaky dribs of red wine for my glass.

Four O' Clock

What stayed after visits from grandparents
Were necktie stiff and mimed to a fetish,
Inhibiting my brute utterance
For "chat" with some deliberation.
Tea was everywhere. That made it British.
Custard on Sunday a sort of house tradition.

Rudy by wool one's flesh goosed up
Shouldered in breathless silk.
A book on herbs rinsed the same cup.
Gracious frowned through a shy grin
At spoons of sugar and spots of milk
Preferring a dulcet of mandarin.

That was important. Then the rex
Dusted fossils for assembly by the dozens.
(My plain jeans were seamed in Middlesex.)
All cruelty it's been supposed was cast
From our sophistications. The cousins'
Culture was hungry, you know, and fast.

Talk Around Table

Grown, with younger siblings who would grow
Again and again to measure with the pains
They hardly took and were transparent to,
With scrunch nose smirks and Napoleonic frowns

I'd see them chasing sure to surer shadows.
I watched their buoyancy turn earnest and grim,
Taunting tolerance onto others' toes—
Na na na igniting for the name

Or word-stick or word-stone wielded to break
Something intangible into stunned silence.
Bristling. Mother reddened, "Goodness sake.
Get out the soap. Somebody's mouth could use a rinse."

Ever left unspoken, lodged in mind,
Eyebrows were raised to suggest the "smart closet"—
Downstairs with coats for winter shut behind
The door for a few moments, less for thought

Than for the pride you swallowed and left behind
In stings of silence. Minutes in there felt
The gulf of ages in an old clock's hand…
But you returned at father's side, the bell

Of an egg-timer gone off to release you.
Mother wiped your "onions" with a tissue.
Given this meaning the table lumped its word
For the deeper consideration we now shared.

Nobody Touches Me

Dear Buck, thanks for the envelopes with your checks.
I'm moved that we're still so close
After all of the hundreds of thousands of miles
We've put on one another. I feel tired.
Those "concrete bricks" you're resting on lend you class
Enough not to write an eyelet
About the items paid for on my bills.
(Still filing your teeth on that vegetarian diet?)
The cost of prescriptions alone may require loans.
For other screws and bolts I will have to impose
On you. An ankle's plastered. A gauzed wrist sprained.
The ole elbow double jointed. Bones
Than feelings are less stubborn, will mend
With time. And you broke them. Over artichokes.

Needles

Woken

gooseflesh

legs and arms with

out a blanket, pincushion

pricked and blood-flecked like

a bat of eye from Grünewald's Christ

scourged, that bed plumed from

the air, those evergreens I dozed beneath

had points to spare.

The Partner

He wouldn't break the silence with sighs
The way Petrosian did. Or gesture out like Barcza.
Or load the boredom stiff as a statue.
He less calculated than pondered
With his concentration over the board
Thickening in the waking winter dark
And the checker 'd go watery beneath the pieces—
Your knight in stirrups at the toe of his pawn.
You'd catch yourself up from a nod and swear
He had left the room. But he kept murmuring at you.
All the while he sat right there
Across the table, not saying a word.

Blue

Across the sky moved much uncertainty.
No better reason to call it the weather.
Whether or not it rained you wore the day
And in the wind were blown sure as a feather,
Determined as the snow to mound then melt
From freeze stung form under a different sun.
Let anybody ask you how you felt
In that pilgrim warmth of spring—to untwist one
Precocious light bud, bait for the frost…
The metaphors of the sky overtook your head's
Transparency, each wandering patch erased
By the recurrence of the wind and clouds
Casting the light in flux mutatis mutandis
Under Wednesday's zodiac, then Thursday's…

The Orchard

Trees stood all winter like cattle in the field
Naked of their leaves in wind and snow,
Their extremities advanced like blind men reading
Braille from the lines of wind that made them tremble.

To look at them for long you would remember
How superficial winter's hardest freeze
Compared to their roots deep as the cemetery's
Shelter where uncles seasoned herring stew.

Dull-lidded looks as I walked home from school
With no more than a candle's wit myself
Shook a head of disparagement at these
Wastes of nature, counting them for dead

Blind to another evening I would wake
To wafts of blossoms through the open window
Recalling wicker baskets. I could see
The swells of ripening in their fingers ache.

Snow

Out of a zillion cat's coughs in the cold
Dry winter evening, I tried to weep
And flurried through mountain fog across the land
Tightening the river in a bed
Of glass. Rolled up by woolen hands I held
This stacked ball-shaped triad with a steep
Chin tucked under a carrot nose. My hand
From a broom head's straw could not tap my head
To think how firmly packed too, too soon thaws
The form of purest stuff away from its form.
The long night crystallizes a day's wink.
Talk of catharsis the next day as I sink
Down for the glares of atmosphere in warm
Steaminess about the man I was.

The Miracle Worker in Work Clothes

With pearl hooks and buttons piecing the Oshkosh
Overalls over the damp denim shirt
Buttoned to the collar and the wrists,
Sweating with reins gripped in calloused hands
Guiding the wide-rump horses and the plow
Across the fields in the warming sun
With the creases of leather boots clumped in clay
The miracle worker
Has raised the dead at Saint Galen's
While the family wept and praised the lord their god.
Like earth stunning
Winter back into spring, the miracle worker
Tensed, a body of sweat and breath, breast borne open
To the holy spirit
With great concentration pushing, pushing
The dead back into this life while men
Looking on stood dumb and amazed
Some of them fainting as the corpse
Shivered squirming, spurting
The blood of life onto the near assistants, then
Gasped and wailed that other
Worldly protest in the constricted
Gagvoice of a summer insect
Chirring, bawling, demonically
Accusing the gathered for having summonsed it
Back to this air.

Go on home, the miracle worker
Shouts at the men still looking on.
The good book sayeth, 'The dead shall be raised'.
I have these fields to plow this morning.

Miller Moths

Late in the summer night and with the heat
This blizzard in the lamps along the street.

A Summer's Day

i.

Blooms of iris on a day in June
Make languid fingers. Stirred in air they join

Or seem to at a pen's movements writing
This, then that, between lifts, hesitating

Silences for margins that acquaint
The arguments of wanderer and saint.

ii.

Disguised for freedom's doubts, one mind debates
Acquired contradictions through the streets

Of a modern city. Its novel industry
Skims comforts, rituals, to moon with poetry

That yarns ten thousand nights into a day's
Meanderings back through his pains and joys.

iii.

The beaten horse vrooms on. So summer can
Google the legends to deathship printout. Man.

Meriwether Lewis

His need, the unexplored, a land unscathed
By European languages, thundered
Dauntingly, understandably
If equivocally upon the ocean
Of the prairie, to boats narrowly
Welcome on its unusual lateral rivers.
The virgin tall grass shuddered to be seen
As the land's mind the sky streamed in the water
Humming under them. From their deeper shade
The great conifers sprang into the 19th century
Authorized by a purchase from the Emperor,
Each ridge of forest as novel as Circe's island
To the old song again. When he shot a bear
Its cave sighed pregnant with the first death.
When they ate bear the moon looked an arched bow
The other way, the river then a blind trickle, the stars
To clusters appearing and appearing, one
By one as far as he could see and now
Although they formed the same eternal
Constellations, this night one of them streaking
Fell from creation to be seen by him.

In his Dream a Horse makes Sense

He is Swift. That is, he is Gulliver
On the final island of his travels
Drawn into the curious signatures
Of horses. Under their nods and shakes of mane,
Neighing and hoofing with wide views to each side
Composed and reasonable they speak
As the superior animals they are
Outward and inward with implicit trust
That sees no use for fiction, for saying that which
Is not, if not exactly. May as well, we are told,
Leave your interlocutor in greater
Ignorance. And yet, dear Swift, is it
Merely a flight of fancy to swallow
That horses could converse with men
Reasoning with us? Okay, they have met
In a place of men. And I have felt your
Disappointment with the Yahoos
Climbing trees to shout down
On a hapless newcomer because he appears
Sophisticated in his shoes and vest
As one possessed of a tongue that would speak
Of honey and roses without mentioning
Bees or thorns. In his dream a silence
Made sense with the real presence, otherness of a horse,
Its stamp and hide's scent in the dusty hay
With large teeth grinning to tell him
It wasn't smiling, that he should keep
His palm cupped flat raising the oats up to
The eerie protrusion of its leathery lip.
You shouldn't even think the thought
Of challenge in the hot breath of its sudden snort,
Of any misgiving
Yours to cast and be received
Tense to the tension, in that deeply figured mirror.

Snowflake

With ghosts of breath fog, need's time must
Embrace
Some cold, other to touch. The sharp air leaks
Progressive brittle
Crystals into akin-to stuff, fluff,
Frost spiked exfoliate form.
Moist humors drive it from this tip,
This tongue, as from a tech smart chip
Onto your flesh flushed warm
Having beheld uniqueness. Enough
Even this little
Prisms (green, yellow) in blinked lashes, streaks
Down your face,
Melting mote of winter dust.

All Business

Demand for supply replaces the accord
From thee to me as our walk down the wood
Blots invention taking inventory
Forgoing our book with eyes wide for a volume

Little more true or heedful than flirtatious
Novels aimed at nest wrens in their straw,
Than witches with effigies or David in a shoe store.
I'm your spin drug, blares the fuzzy song

Of flushed notes in accelerated rhythms
Under Mercury's lyre stuffed in headphones
Prompting rapid keys, disintegrating
The vertiginous virginal blank page

With thoughts set in the sand of editsoft.
As atmosphere conditions, as winter dooms us,
This 24/7 culture circles to compel
Night and day to vigilance for a deadline

Again deferred like loans one fine day pays
From the elusive rainbow's pot of gold
With a ring for Cassandra Salviati's hand.
My pen is gnawed. My cup is of disposable foam.

Sense for a Stockbroker

His leather briefcase
May as well hold
Archimedes'
Standard for gold.

Each day what he does
Nudges the market
And somehow weighs
In everybody's pocket

With his points and margins
Quoting a price
That makes sense
Like a hand in ice.

Sometimes you glance
With a frown
At his lines of poetry
Arrowed up and down

Across the bottom
Of the pub's big screen.
The whole cake in crumbs.
It is obscene

With his insomnia figured
Into the brim
Dilution of my coffee.
I don't get through to him.

Daisy Miller

No object to her life but days to fill
In an old busy manner that betrayed
Her father's fortune was a novelty,
Even at tea she just could not sit still.
Her fingers were nervous, the lace at her sleeve cuffs frayed.
Time bothered her skirt's pleats, time and gravity.

There was so very much to see in Rome
Haunted to wonder whatever does one *do*
When seated for a visit, sat to watch
For the host to come into the drawing room.
The ruins were very old and that was true.
Raphael accomplished so very much.

Her peers in the hotel lobbies read their books.
They were instructed. They really passed the time.
It was important to be literary.
Whatever was a mirror for but one's looks.
Clutched to her plume, Daisy set out to tame
The day's anxiety with an itinerary.

Meeting appointments was another thing
Entirely, not just by a lady's whim
But deeper matters of incident and fate
That lost sense of an hour in the evening.
The sun sets before things actually go dim.
She could be late. She could be fashionably late.

Sparrows and Starlings

Seen mingled on the sidewalk
They contend for crumbs of bread
And beg to be compared.
Under human feet that tread
Sparrows skip, haughty starlings stalk—
The daring and the dared..

Differences in a shared place
Mind their manner, size for size.
Little sparrows flinch
Soon as the lordly starling flies
To their noisy gathering, curious
To know what's tossed from a nearby bench.

Though the sparrows jump away
They are sudden to return
Adding at a glance
Numbers against the starling's scorn.
Now its singular awkward tyranny
Becomes the object of their *presence*.

Dabs of others' beaks divert
The concentration of one's own.
Dabs of others' beaks
Dart at wrappers, every sort
Of twig and butt that should be left alone.
It's hard to read between the cracks

Of bricks where grass and thistles crop.
Clever starlings, when they must,
When feisty sparrows swarm,
Preen themselves in lowly dust,
Bow and crouch and even seem to hop
And in this other covert form

Vie with them whom parable
Reputes as wanting worryfree birds.
Will they accept this fellow?
Experience must prove words.
At provision's nods, our being is bearable,
Sparrows inspired, starlings stellar.

Day Moon

Endless whirr now in a sleepless window
Lovers' path lamp—

Masked inconspicuous now in the pale blue
Light of the day's sky, in whose bee hum
The mirror of the mind keeps full and thoughtless
For this oddity of boundaries crossed
Like spring in winter, that lonely
Orbit nearly consumed
By its greater farther so partial reflection.

Ghost Man

We kids together with our shirts off came
That end of summer morning on the path
Around the grove on toward the bridge and found him
Lying beneath a tree, at first mistaking him
For one of the men who camped by the train yard
Sleeping off a drunk. Closer up
Something was worse than we'd expected.
My young body reacted doubling over
Elbows at my groin where I had cramped
Trying to run to keep up with the others
Heading back for town to find the adults.

The rope had been cut from the tree. The papers
Spoke of homicide, while others thought
Another had found him there and let him down
Then fled, fearing misunderstanding.

His death left unresolved, our finding ripened
In my imagination. Any time
I came back to the bridge his ghost arose—
Rematerializing from that valley
Of dead bones into another presence
Half-there of my own mind and fear and out
For vengeance for my having been among
The living who had witnessed his corpse,
Half-there of his own residual being,
The monument he'd left, man for a man.

Repeatedly I hated his love
Of getting me to hate him. While the novelty
Of his decomposition granted itself passage into
The mole-hill mountains of my mind, I hated
Dreading the intensity of his one opened eye
Enlarging you in its focus. I was alone
In the labyrinth and deep shadows of the woods
With nowhere to run to, nowhere to hide.

His nose was wrinkled pug, turned up in defiance.
The dark smoke of his one eye could see straight through you.

The worn knuckles of his two left fingers
Gave away his four-point gait
With the thick balance and complexity
Of odors surrounding him.

He had a weird hermetic energy
And marathon runner's stamina as he leaped
From tree to tree grabbing onto the branches
Where he'd hang his weight, seeking the dead
Limbs that would tumble down with him.

Around his scented area here and there
He dug out holes and thatched them with twigs
Forming in ties the line of a long trail
Camouflaging it with leaves. We'd heard
Of sightings of a deer, its leg broken in
One of the pits, bunched in a nimbus of flies
Staring out of sockets (eaten by crows)
Up through the weft of bright September woods—
A visible sign of death humbling
The pride of the fallen stag's pointed rack,
The ghost man's trophy, to reward his heeding
This call to raise decay that went on silently
To the trumpet-form and phallic fungi
Blown in rotted logs and under mulch,
Some of them edible, some of them toxic.
I wondered if he knew the difference though.
He bedded for several days under the bridge
Not far from the deer's corpse that lay half-buried
Under a makeshift tomb of beaded holly.
Day after day exhausted there he slept
With matted hair, an untrimmed beard like Cocteau's
Beast waiting for Beauty to take him in her arms
And resurrect his princely smooth chin—
As stories would have it. It was enough for me
To see the thick cage of his chest still breathing,
Not bothering to poke him with the branch I held,

Backing away with the impression of him
Unconsciously moving a long finger nail
Scratching through the stones and sticks and dirt,
Confirming for me the dead man was still alive.

Some days later, he'd be there again
Barring my passage to the pathway bridge.
For hours after I'd given up and turned
Away from that crossing with its graceful camber
Over the river, he followed me
In silence, appearing behind a large stone
Or from a hedge or through a row of trees—
The knotted hunch over to one shoulder
For his abandoned judgment, the missing teeth
Sure sign he had no fear and would eat anything
Even a grown kid's finger. Till late at night
I lay breathless and tensed seeing his echo still,
Trapped in the dread of the next day's
Demand again for me to try the bridge
Braced in coal smoke wood with iron railings.
The bank at the other shore was dense in foliage.
A dark pool of placid water at the concrete pillars
Breathed rings and finned the glass with trout—
As ideal as grass over the hill, and that improbable.
Each day as I approached with sudden
Howls and raspy grunts from his tight windpipe
He leapt from his new place or out of the blue
Dropped from a thick branch overhead to land
Exactly in my way, with no way around him.
I couldn't outrun him but ran all the same
Day after day, only to avoid
The occasion of violence that seemed inevitable.
The ghost man with his hostility and determination
Like water heeding gravity through a worn shingle
Devastated all fleeting resolutions
On how to lock the doors to my awareness.

Any time I sat down by myself
To let my mind be back away from things
In the sharp chirr of locusts or wind in leaves

With my fishing line gone slack in esses on the water
Downstream a safe ways from the bridge
A stillness would gather, then to be accused
By the constant hum of traffic back and forth
Up over the hill along the four-lane with
An outlet mall and dealerships and restaurants.
You should be doing something. Don't just sit here.

Already half an hour and the fish weren't biting.
Overhead a hawk held wide wings spread
Wheeling on updrafts, overlooking me—
Signaling my presence to others nearby
Attracting the ghost man eager to get
His nails on the rodent or pigeon of the hawk's hunt
To tear at with is his odd tooth, spitting out the fur and feathers.

At some point back near town along the roofs
Thickening into the neighborhood he'd left off
Following me, annoyed at the chorus
Of howling dogs of the living that paced the yards' fences.

Now all was quiet, with stars flagged in the window,
A hook of moon, autumn gusts rustling
In the dry arbor. I could feel my throat swallow—
I lay that quiet. Waiting for sleep to come.
Near my limit, forgetting he was out there somewhere.

Then a stick snapped outside the house. I could hear
Or thought I heard that cough or grunt of his
Ducking in the shadows I peered at through the window
Seeing things, doubting my sight, his power
There or not there to have me looking for him.

Hand Me Downs

My brother's length bunched denim at my ankles
Although I notched them tight, high at the hips,
The belt of stitched leather with an uncle's
Name burned across the back between the loops.
The hollow fingertips of dad's work gloves
Pinched to my stubby reach in thawing frost
From hard to get a hold of autumn leaves
That piled up here—then fluttered there and there.
Little was found that fit, for thank-you mumbled,
Tent shirts that hung down to my knees or past.
I was straw for style. Others were remembered.
Beyond their season things withstood a year
Stretched to casual, wear tear, raggedy,
Nearly familiar, for me or anybody.

Zeno's Hero

The diffidence I called calm,
Impatience I called courage,
The difference of your wit,
If not wisdom, to be rejected
With a resigned spite
Pitching your voice in irony
To tell me to go ahead.
You're still standing. (On a raindrop.)

Achilles after the tortoise,
Twice as fast as other
Halving the close each stride
Could only halve, never close
The patience of his opponent—
A truth in paradox?
Now I could term *a* definition
For the prayer I didn't have.

Dour Larkin
for Brian Mitchell

Everything wrong, the awful pie he ate,
The apple for the basket to the floor.
What's our pleasure reading his defeat
If not for the resilience of his humor
Left in tact, despite some very strange
Crabbing from events he couldn't change?

There is a sort of dim transparency
Aboard the Whitsun train of grooms and brides
Meditating the bachelor's jealousy.
Or is he sour to be on that ride's
Promise of new grass over each next hill
Mindful mostly of the terminal

And all that luggage he chose not to pack?
Summering with his mother, in soliloquy
Pecking at Hamlet from Horatio's cloak—
Tongue in cheek, knowing the average guy
Wanted his winter hand in just a glove,
That we may love what doesn't exact our love.

Uncle Uncle

"Give unk a big hug," lurching he would say
With his large work hands clamped to my breathless ribs.
I wanted desperately to get away.
The dry breath of milk coffee. And those rubs
Of stubble that would redden on my face.
His knuckles shuffling through my parted hair.
What was the magic word to obtain grace?
Mom and dad were laughing. It wasn't fair.
It isn't fair. I sit here now. The page.
The phrase I try again sounds...off—or flat.
I squirm and want to get up. "Just budge—
Try to escape," he taunts me. "Go on and write."

Surplus Soldier

A "Geneva man in recovery" he now knows
Whatever he crossed eyes at in those Eastern dozes
Used to magnetize his imperfections. Now it doesn't.
Now his service has contracts in the garden
Of the kind of general acceptance
He once thought his exclusive exertion, now his receipt.

He stands at a chalkboard holding dangerous chalk.
His students are his enemies: to learn
A rule 's as good as seeing its villages smolder,
Its women raped, its reservoirs sieved
When silence the Keeper is sabotaged by chit-chat.
People freeze when everything's explained

In forward diction bundled in their pockets.
You could squat in black arm bands, just for the rush,
Like Odysseus for toxic arrowheads
Trade and look the other way, running
For your freedom in a hamster wheel.
Then your worst enemy is cynicism,

The world so objectively torn apart
The sense inside your head becomes everything
Heedless of the animate world's stings
Or drops of honey, inconsiderate of hints
Imagined…heard, skipping here in your pledge.
Then you can have your bullets. Are there any questions?

Wednesday Slider

All for a Wednesday morning beaded in dew
And you are left out, to have to think so hard,
Be shriveled by the ubiquitous regard
Of your people's indignation. Go ahead and dangle
Metaphors. I mean, really. Just who
Do you think you are? Ever seen a real jungle?...

The Imposter

He's a weatherman who sees tomorrow's rain
And doesn't think of an umbrella.
Weirdly aware he isn't made of
Salt, he is unlike the rest of us
In that he doesn't panic when it showers.
He'll wrinkle a suit, won't run for cover.
He is an old sailor. In northern gale or temperate westerly
The sea is the sea, as a child
Behaved or terrible is ever a mother's child.
Like us, though, he gets caught in the rain
Without his umbrella. Unlike us
The merely incidental in hindsight, days later,
Torments him to remorse. We were only forgetful.

When it's one of us instead of the rain
And he is caught off guard, he calls his own bluff
Saying "sorry" at least once into hollowness,
A half a teaspoon sweet, on the brink
Of unnerving you in his attempt to placate.
You hadn't even minded being called "very natural."
But now you start to. What might "very natural" mean
Now that he "didn't mean *exactly very* natural"?
What did that mean?

He has a deep hobby (comic books
Or calculus) that resounds in his head
Throughout the day, confusing you
As drawn too simply, too intricately factored
Into a complex equation.

If you wondered
What he knew about you anyway
It would give him an edge
You could not acknowledge
Secretly in his likeness.

Armenia

Juniper, sloe, dog rose and honeysuckle
Dab the semidesert where narrow streams trickle.

Hawks and gophers fabled a lexical
Countryside that could have been New Mexico—

In moments adrift in silence, hot wind and sun.
Near any village more permanent civilization

Hovered in dust and wear in the mountain rocks,
Oddness of mason churches and delivery trucks.

I'd sneak a lemonade or Hershey bar between hazards
At customizing my sweet tooth on dates and mazzards.

In Yerevan, Sayat, a student and flat-mate
Showed me the letters of their alphabet, all thirty-eight—

To be remembered in beginner's Greek
Through pages, to make myself encyclopedic.

Forbidden Furniture

With pinecones, acorns, dropped pennies in a trail,
Crests of old roots revealing
Desire dreamt in earth's erosion,
The unfathomable patience of her life veins
Move more freely, even to be removed,
Cut down and taken and sawed and cut again,
Planed and notched and polished, as you've dreamt
Your way into becoming a mother of poor children
Scrubbing floors down on all fours until
This chair that sits on you shifts its hams
And leans forward with its elbow toward the desk
As to a rural cry of timber, tingling
To what would be the heels you stood upon,
Pair after pair of shoes having worn into
The ruin of your feet. Until they let
The rain in, these you wear can only be tied
Again with the same taste of morning coffee,
Full of character, rankled legerdemain
For the promise this will one day change
To ask more than a sign for. There are signs.
Promises. To maintain delays. Preserve
The secrets. Scent of onions on the grill.
But it won't change while you can't think it will.
Pulled from a lake you nearly drowned in once
You loved the air your father and the earth
And kept your gate as you would keep your heart
Free of the snake's envies and frustrations.
There's no interest in your neighbors' honesty.
Their smiles are facetious and endowed
With toilet paper their kids toss into your tree.
You leave it flagging up there over the hedge
You've busied yourself to trim, the walk you've swept—
Shrugging to take the joke, to show you can.

Psyche

Butterfly, fellow of unseen lover,
Beauty to the Beast,
Intangible one deeply to suffer,
The mind is a terrible thing to waste.

Pearl of price a thousand years the mimics
Reached for as sexual
Apple of your eye lucky to last two weeks,
Flood light pride descent of angel

Player of this music: help make
Me move again, the lost prince lift
To a new promise, mirror in the dark,
Bride dressed for her burial, curse, gift.

Who Are these People?

Autumn people in the day-round harvest
Work, encompassed by a gold of grain
They hardly account for, with their interest
Hurried to bundle sheaves. The painter has

Given an envious eye to the rich light
Engulfing the vague ragdoll portraits of
These Adam's children at their toil, the fat
Bent-over rumps, stuffed shirts and rolled-up sleeves

Busily negligent of sympathetic
Summer still life, poultry, fruit and cheese,
The character of laggards with their drink,
Worn of time in an old pair of shoes

That make you wonder where their kids come from.
Their hands are gloves. A world only imagined
Remote and left behind, though surely the same
Familiar actors, in this different pageant.

From the Kitchen Window

By lantern light potatoes in the kitchen
Peel and fall to pieces under a knife
Into a sink of water. They will fry
When the men are in the barn milking the cows
But only with their coffee in them first.

With early chores done they will break the fast
Night observed sleeping, posed in death
Whose icon with hollow ribs grossly grins
Out of allegorical paintings in the books
From school days. Then she dreamed that she would leave
This speechless land of crop fields and hog pens
And travel the roads with Cather to the cities.

The strange intimacy of
Dreams has never left her. Like the bulbs
Of tulips on the morning side of the house
Ghosts sleep all through her winter to surprise her waking.
After the snow has melted one warm morning
There like little fingers, green dead flesh,
The leaves of tulips reach out from their graves
With their one task to pull the bloom's head up.

With her hands busy and a mind of winter streams
All to herself this quiet hour no clock's
Hand plays its ruse for the chirring of the crickets,
A pulse that ebbs then rises back again
Then ebbs, widening, waiting for the shapes
Of buildings and equipment to step forth
Into their gray appearances. The landing
Of dawn's far first light like gentle mist

Fluffed, gradual to a pin's point, jars the cock's
Sleep to a crowing it crows before it has woken
Or realized the day had ever
Drained from the vigil of its roost
Equal to the sun.

Season of Fever

Blame the season, spring, bud in youth's mouth
To bloom brilliantly against the age
Old foot of root stepped up around the oak
Whose trunk has known the hands of children climbing,
The dog's sniff and its lifted leg; his tie
Firm at the collar to his pulse of life—
And heart the squirrel that thrives in the oak's blood,
That lithe, that gray and that elusive.

The gallants are still transparent to the shifty
Weather of March, sallies of morning sun
And sudden glooms of showers. They shade with this
Inconstancy to which the snoop
Polonius can only be mock-hearted
With no stomach for the beef they crave.

And when it frosts a late spring night in May not
Any of us are ignorant
Or unmoved by the little deaths of blossoms
And fruits this year taken for granted.

Nana Marie

Waftably slight of frame and tougher than nails
The maiden in her didn't care to cut
That forest she tamed braids of in her hair.
Hay-spun gleaming braids hung from the loft
Of a fairytale she read to me in bed
As I dozed in a vision of my want
For let-downs from somewhere
Unlikely and disregarded as a barn—
Coming upon the weft of silent thought
That could be spun into sketchy plots
With their sketchy characters, a spice witch fishing
For your trout, ogres at their bridges
And a goose whose egg contained the map
To Cato Darwin, that last one you meet
At the gate of world's end, waking from your rest.
Their costumes in the wind you would remember
Until you needed their disarray of truths
Like the shroud the shrewd widow unwove again
And again, waiting for her gone seaman's return.
With combed silk spooled from her sewing box
Nana Marie eyed needles to mend our buttons,
Her finger in the care of a shiny thimble
Against the prick that threaded the hem's seams.
She was and was not there then was again
The warm and singing voice my waning followed
Yawning, puzzled for (breath on candle) what dreams.

Summer

The whole long season a moment
consensually a culture ceases to resonate
with the thaws of dawn because the days are longer
and most are dressed in shorts. Few
wait in school cafeteria lines. We skirt
the margins of the lake's shores and don't want
the ample breaths of rye and thyme
on our sandwiches. It speaks
in the disguises of columns and quotes
for verses. Its different voice whispers
scrimmaging with meaning still read
between the lines, for countersense, if it's true
that poetry is ethical, until the old craving
has the trees decide
to shed again,
woods in their stillness and solitude
when the camps are shut down and the motor
boats desert the lakes to the geese.
So long till then. Though you made fair sense
reading Wyatt to be read
for ear and classroom, memory, it's summer
working down and across in close squints now.

Cute Tyrant

Sure, it's a story. But you want to tell him
About the fabric of this robe he wears.
It's not the pearl eyelet waist-high in the seam
Of terrycloth we would wince at to see torn
Let alone wrinkled, which he takes for granted,
That wants to break your deep complicity
With those in the entourage who oo and ah
As much to keep their heads as his crown up.
Sure, it's odd. My chin has seldom dropped
As shocked by paradox at this spectacle
Of people entertaining the illusion
That he is valued more precisely for
Exposing himself in our postured flaws,
Frayed sleeves, the tear in the pocket hem
Where the toy hands have improvised a niche.

You want to lean your pencil toward the margin
And draw yourself, a stickman with an exclamation mark
For thought—and dash of finger pointing at him,
His exposure tingling on your tongue, when you
First sense their floating eyes back from the page
Shifting toward you with their expectations
Sizing you in the draft that snugly fit him.

A Label Lacks the Wearer's Character

The trouble is to live for labels at least
One simple as a shirt size, when you barely
Fit into a whole closet full of shirts.

Worse to be a daylight person when the night falls,
A coat-and-tie person on the beach.
Worse yet a people person as the lone

Survivor of a plane crash on a frozen
Arctic island in a herd of penguins
Asking for rests of krill and books of matches.

All of our lives we're told to be something
Only to find our chosen occupation
Comes with a hazard, machinist's carpel-tunnel,

Lab assistant's exposure, tennis pro's
Elbow… The trouble is to take a label
Once and for all and stitch it to that changing

Fabric of me, *me* you cannot shed,
I and thou netting in the paradoxes,
To dive on one's behalf, yet not indulge in shellfish.

Keeper's Scorn

I will go to the bank by the wood and become undisguised and naked...
— 'Song of Myself'

The branches to the path into the forest
Swished behind me. Closed. I was alone
Where trees dropped nuts for squirrels and sparrows bathed
In standing water from the wide winds' rains,

Where weasels climbed to linnets' nests for eggs.
Up from the stream's bank lay a pair of boots
Of well-stitched tanning. I was alone
To slip out of old sneakers into them—

My left foot scraping something in the heal
Of that fine folded leather. Reaching in
I found the photographs in plastic sleeves,
Family members, with some business cards,

One of them reading *A. Ford Givens Surplus,*
Another *Carmon's Photography...* A pair
Of orange foot-fitted socks had been left
Beside the boots. I could see nobody

Either way of the current, just a coyote
Surprising a crow from the fruit pulp of a skin
In the thatched view through branches on a hill
Across the stream. To blinds going east and west

Ghosts trickled rising footsteps from the water
Good as no minding present, all around,
Above the crow still circling in the air
Unsatisfied to leave its competition

Below with the cluster of its diligent meal.

Seeing me walk away sore footed still
The coyote was distracted, lifting its glowing
Mouth from the hare, as though it were not there.

It could outwait some silence for the threat
I posed to it. As soon as other crows began
Cawing at the unevenness of my step
From heaven knew where, hunger buried its face again

And I knew, the ignorant are blessed
In their allowance to relish all oncoming
Traffic to the abrupt and bittersweet
Boundaries of given spaces, while

Conscience like a bat at twilight casts its sense
To map the contours of danger that surround
Its flight, creator and abider of
This pledge not to run into anything.

Crying in the Rain

The sky stoops to us to feel
The way we feel sometimes.
Given the role, sometimes the fool
In me no best intention tames,

Not the reasons I would be right
Unwrong me or convince your blue
To see always only on the bright.
I'm less than what I *have to* do

Now that the sky has opened; below
You hear an old voice soften from
The elements that ply a willow
And the rain's long fingers' fretted strum.

Berries

Now and then you could taste
Autumn in the berries
A wee bit tart for your
Pucker that ran to the cave
Of your throat, watering
Your whole mouth. Even your gums
Ached in the sworn fruit's savor,

Pungent to tears the scent
That blossomed through the palate
Hung on a limb of the mind
To be picked a second
Time as the split to open
Gift with the tooth-crooked seeds
For her who taught grammar trees

And numbers and rule
To floating pupils.
What were you learning
Gazing up at her
Missing a sentence?

Now You're a Soprano, Louisa Solano
the 20th of June, 2008

There comes a time
to preserve a place
from its neglect
in the abandon of anonymity,
a progress of circles

as they go on to live by criticism
who didn't
bother so much over themselves
as others.

Now the occasion says so, with brevity
in shy honor to bear our levity

though you have mattered these years around the Square
and Cambridge means to keep you with your name there.

Anne à Versailles

The drive to see your parents stops for coffee.
You ask if I'm going to be awful. I can be
Sweetened. The packs open. Stirrers swirl.
I vow my goodness for their little girl
And you say fairy tales are partially true.
I used to listen with my fingers curled
Dreaming some paradise. Now you
Sense what the clouds of heaven do to the world.

People drift across the café window
Back and forth to show where I can go
When my coffee's empty, while the sunlight
Beams in from the street. There's more to write
Because completed things, if fiddle-faddle,
If even in the least, bring thoughts to settle

Much as creation lets them, each animal
Named to the very particles that make it.
These moments find the garden close and small
Enough to tolerate our naked
Knowledge. In their spun obedience
They argued plain sense senseless at its word,
Our parents' generation, wise and with scorn,
Already in 1960, on this day
As scientists eyed the moon, and you were born
To make our lives happier anyway.

A Summer Pasta for Eunice

Strangely familiar, common for sublime
Savors that gather back a whole lifetime,
   Butterflies and penne, elbows carry
Substance to the vinaigrette our loaves
Break in to dab up aubergines and olives—
   August (a breath) with parsley and rosemary.

Unchained Sonnet

We lingered late for classes watching kids
Sail boats across the fountain, the clock
Of minutes then another dove, unmelted
In the desert sun, before it was stuffed
To shift hands on a wall, days
That were not perfect but as now
Will be better when edited,
Once they sound right, certain
The next temptation for a different choice
Will dream back into the margins of older books
With garden vines and beasts of fable,
Hare and tortoise, fox and crow and cheese
And cow, the illustrations of
Creation's reasoning. Maybe I had reached
The end of novelty. No less perhaps
My risk and pleasure, when one veered for me,
Stepped off a curb without checking both ways.
It happens. You look up. This lady trying
To jump out of a car (and it happens fast)
Changes her mind. You hear the car door slam
And see again the look she gave you. Satan was weeping.
Our names were written in a common dye
Readers of news take home on their hands.
The earth had shaken. You were through the light.

In and Out

Sudden of foot
chilled in the season—
to trace its flight breathing
plumes

obeying no reason
that would determine you
for your detriment
as music played Mozart,
as painting Van Gogh
thinly pulled out before our eyes

that blind to me
you, air, ubiquitous
and inconspicuous
I name the stuff of sighs.

Changing the Direction of a Train

The long freight train passed by each night
Drowning the wait of silence in
Our trailer-house, a field's length from
The railroad tracks. It drowned the field
In tremors that shook a club-hand clock
And picture frame on the little stand
Beside my bed tingling in response
To the massive weight of the freight cars.
It traveled west to east from a phrase
Of my father's, "bringing
The earthquakes with it." Though in my mind
Waking from a doze at the cry
Of its whistle and thunder herding past
It had to be determined on the way
Of the world, chasing the sun, humming
Me back to sleep before it had gone
Around the bend and up into the mountains.

While the Umpire Sang

In dreams you have a place to stand in there
Watching things come at you like that first
Ball from the pitcher arcing for your head
Which when you flinch and duck and crouch away
Snaps in the thick leather of the catcher's mitt
Squarely over home plate, and as from nowhere
Stee-riike the umpire blind behind you
Booms out for the whole stadium to hear
Followed by a crescendo of cheers down on you.

With deep breaths swinging your bat, to show you can,
You sense behind you a shuffling of flesh-like wings
Settle, and the pitcher on his hill there
Nods in assent to the conspiracy
He has with these two masked men at the plate,
Motioning in his windup, then the shoulder
Turns and in less than a second here it comes
An instant floating, straight down the middle
For the fat of your swing—a little high?—
And though your body starts forward in the swing
Your wrists pull back no sooner than to regret
The crazy flapping of a voice above you, screeching
Tw-hoo echoing *Bravo! Bravo!*
Like a lead pendulum in the cast iron
Bell of your head that shakes the wide-lobed helmet.
You stand away to tap your cleats free
Of the red clay of the batter's box, to unstrap
Then tighten the Velcro of your damp gloves
Holding the bat out in a deliberate even
Half-swing to show that you are still in control.
Down the third-base line the coach signals to you
With nods of his cap rim and brushes on his forearms.
You step back into the deepened chalked box now
With no doubt still whether to take or swing away

But just with the next pitch in a vast starry
Darkness from above the stadium lights
A vague quilt stuffed with flight descends on you
Pinning the pine bat stiff against your chest
With the vampire bat settled thereupon
Tearing at your fingers on the grip tar—
All of a second of a held breath lasting
Out of time, until you struggle free
Gasping finally with your hands clenched choking
A pillow to death, shaking it against the wall…

Then in the calm, with things in the dark room
Settled back into themselves, a fresh breeze sighing
Through the window, you allow flickers
To come back to you of that steep dream
With the lighted green field, cheers of the remote spectators,
The scoreboard flashing innings and the outs,
The organ music, complicity of glances
Under caps, the dugout with your teammates there,
And that last pitch starting from the reliever's fist
That failed to meet your timing—or misjudgment…

How was it called? Did you go down swinging? Did you walk?

Reservations

The scent of closer coffee in the house.
The pillow and the gravity it has.
The growl inside the belly for its bacon.
The bathroom scale, its needle and your scan.
The office that might miss you for a day.
The break room rumors quiet, poignant, petty...

All still in question with what hay you're making.

ABOUT THE AUTHOR

Michael Todd Steffen's poetry has appeared in *Connecticut Review,
ACM (Another Chicago Magazine), Ibbetson Street* and *Wilderness House
Literary Review.* From his BA in Literature and French at Belmont in
Nashville, on a Rotary International Fellowship he took his MA
in Northern Renaissance Studies at Sussex in Brighton, England,
going on to teach in France and translate Ronsard throughout
the 1990s. He currently writes, and works for non-profits, living
between Cambridge and Waltham, Massachusetts.

www.ingramcontent.com/pod-product-compliance
Lightning Source LLC
Chambersburg PA
CBHW031006090426
42737CB00008B/708